Consultants

Crystal Hahm, M.A., Ed. M.
Tustin Unified School District

Bijan Kazerooni, M.A.
Chapman University

Publishing Credits

Rachelle Cracchiolo, M.S.Ed., *Publisher*
Conni Medina, M.A.Ed., *Managing Editor*
Emily R. Smith, M.A.Ed., *Series Developer*
June Kikuchi, *Content Director*
Susan Daddis, M.A.Ed., *Editor*
Courtney Roberson, *Senior Graphic Designer*

Image Credits: Image credits: front cover (left) William Philpott/Getty Images, (right) Sergio Del Grande Mondadori Portfolio/Newscom; back cover (right) rook76/Shutterstock; p.5 Watford/Mirrorpix via Getty Images; p.6 World History Archive/Alamy; p.7 (top) Brand X Pictures/Getty Images; p.8 Old Paper Studios/Alamy; p.9 courtesy of U.S. Patent and Trademark Office; p.10 courtesy of National Park Service; p.11, 14, 15 Public Domain; p.13 courtesy of National Library of Medicine; p.18 photo by Marion S. Trikosk, LOC, LC-ppmsc 03265; p.19 360b/Shutterstock; p.20 Jeff Kowalsky/AFP/Getty Images; p.21, 24 Bettmann/Getty Images; p.22 Richard Ellis/AFP/Getty Images; p.23 rook76/Shutterstock; p.25 ITAR-TASS Photo Agency/Alamy; all other images from iStock and/or Shutterstock.

Library of Congress Cataloging-in-Publication Data

Names: Lopez, Elizabeth Anderson, author.
Title: Women who changed the world / Elizabeth Anderson Lopez.
Description: Huntington Beach, CA : Teacher Created Materials, [2019] |
 Includes index.
Identifiers: LCCN 2017053275 (print) | LCCN 2017056493 (ebook) | ISBN
 9781425825591 | ISBN 9781425825171 (pbk.)
Subjects: LCSH: Women--History--Juvenile literature.
Classification: LCC HQ1121 (ebook) | LCC HQ1121 .L665 2019 (print) | DDC
 305.409--dc23
LC record available at https://lccn.loc.gov/2017053275

Teacher Created Materials

5301 Oceanus Drive
Huntington Beach, CA 92649-1030
www.tcmpub.com

ISBN 978-1-4258-2517-1

© 2018 Teacher Created Materials, Inc.
Printed in Malaysia
THU001.48806

D1437661

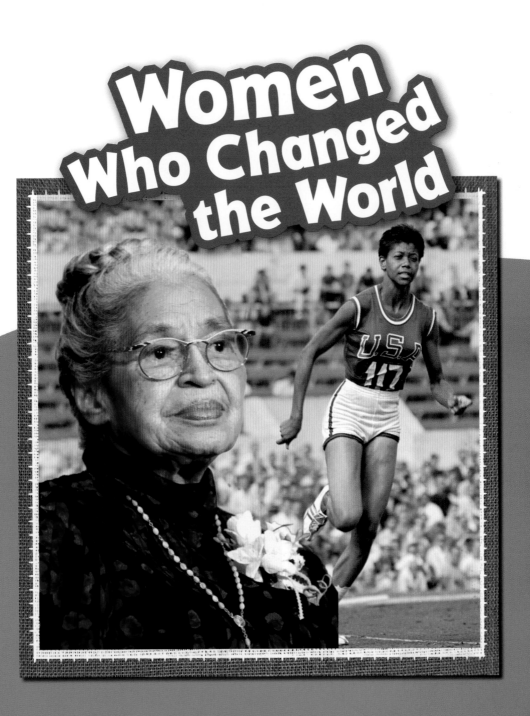

Women Who Changed the World

Elizabeth Anderson Lopez

Table of Contents

Making a World of Difference

Women around the world do great things every day. There are famous women who lead nations. Some women are not well-known, but they still do great things. They make their towns better. They stand up for what they know is right.

There are women who are in charge of huge businesses. Other women help cure people.

It has not always been easy for women. Throughout history, they have had to work hard to succeed.

In the past, women were not allowed to do things that they can today. Some of these things might surprise you. Women could not vote in the United States until 1920.

Women could not open bank accounts. Men had to go with them to the bank. Their husbands or fathers had to allow it. That did not change until 1974. Even schools had rules against girls. They could not go to certain colleges just because they were girls!

Women vote for the first time in Washington, DC.

Many things have changed. Women have changed the world. They have made a difference for people everywhere.

Citizens over the age of 18 in the United States can vote.

Today, a woman can open a bank account on her own.

Women Who Healed

Health care has advanced through the years. Meet two women who changed the world of health in amazing ways.

Clara Barton

Clara Barton

Clara Barton proved you are never too old to do great things. Barton also proved that you could change your path in life. First, she was a teacher. Most teachers back then were men. Later, she worked in the U.S. Patent Office. She was one of the first clerks to work for the government. Barton started to volunteer. She helped get supplies to soldiers in the **Civil War**. Then, she went to help soldiers in person. Some of them were sick or hurt.

Form PTO-1595
OMB No. 0651-0027 (non-Hague exp. 04/30/2015)
OMB No. 0651-0075 (Hague exp. 09/30/2017)

U.S. DEPARTMENT OF COMMERCE
United States Patent and Trademark Office

RECORDATION FORM COVER SHEET
PATENTS ONLY

To the Director of the U.S. Patent and Trademark Office: Please record the attached documents or the new address(es) below.

1. Name of conveying party(ies)

Additional name(s) of conveying party(ies) attached? ☐ Yes ☐ No

3. Nature of conveyance/Execution Date(s):
Execution Date(s) _____
☐ Assignment
☐ Security Agreement
☐ Joint Research Agreement
☐ Government Interest Assignment
☐ Merger
☐ Change of Name

2. Name and address of receiving party(ies)
Name: _____
Internal Address: _____
_____
Street Address: _____
_____
City: _____
State: _____
Country: _____ Zip: _____

Additional name(s) & address(es) attached? ☐ Yes ☐ N

U.S. Patent Office

If you invent something, you want to make sure no one steals your idea. That's why you need a patent. You have to write all the details and file the formal document. That proves the invention was your idea.

After the war, Barton learned more about helping people. In 1881, she started the American Red Cross. She led it for 23 years. The Red Cross still helps people. It helps during times of war. It helps people who have been in **natural disasters**, too.

Clara Barton

Florence Nightingale

Being in the hospital in the 1800s was not the same as it is today. The rooms were not clean. Clothes and sheets were dirty. There was no clean water. This was not safe. Florence Nightingale worked to change that.

Florence Nightingale

Nightingale came from a rich family. No one wanted her to be a nurse. At that time, wealthy women did not work. But it was what she wanted to do. There was a war in the 1850s. Nightingale went to a hospital to help. It was not clean. Some soldiers died from wounds. More died from infections.

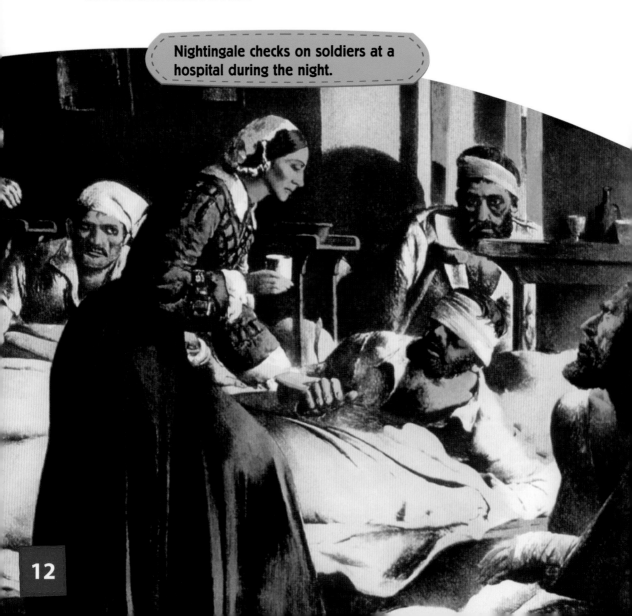

Nightingale checks on soldiers at a hospital during the night.

Nightingale had nurses clean the hospital. She made sure there was clean water. This made it safer for patients.

She **inspired** others to become nurses. Many rich people changed their minds. They now thought being a nurse was a **noble** job.

Paging Dr. Blackwell!

Elizabeth Blackwell earned her degree in medicine. She was the first woman in the United States to do this. Some male students did not think she should be there. But she proved she belonged. In 1849, Blackwell graduated.

Women Who Were First

For years, few women had leading jobs in science or government. These two women worked to change that.

Marie Curie

Marie Curie was born in 1867 in Poland. She was a gifted student. She graduated from high school when she was 15 years old. Next, she wanted to go to college. But girls were not allowed to do this in Poland. So, she moved to France. There, she could go to school. She earned two college degrees in science and math.

Europe in 1860

After college, she went to work in a lab. There, she met Pierre Curie. They worked together and got married.

Marie and Pierre Curie

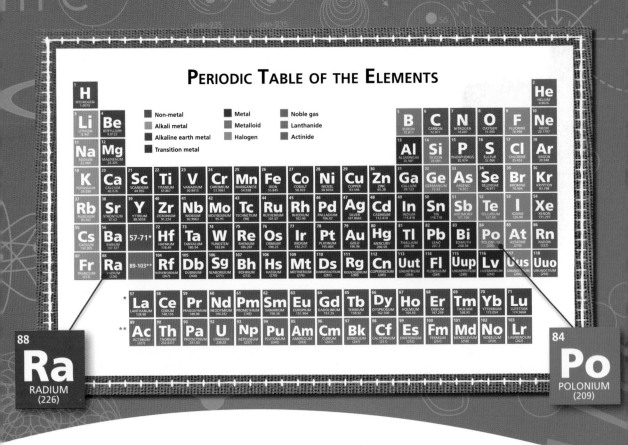

PERIODIC TABLE OF THE ELEMENTS

The Curies discovered two **elements**. They won the **Nobel Prize** for physics. This was the first time a woman won this award. Sadly, Pierre Curie died three years later. Curie was asked to take his place as a teacher at a college. She became the first woman to teach there.

She was also named head of the lab. Eight years after her first win, Curie won the Nobel Prize again. This time, it was for chemistry.

Lots of Prizes

Today, Nobel Prize winners take home a medal and some money, too. They take home over one million dollars!

Curie was famous for her work in the lab. But it made her sick. She died from **leukemia** (loo-KEE-mee-uh). It was caused by **radiation**. Still, her memory lives on. Thanks to her, there are many more jobs in science for men and women.

Golda Meir

Golda Meir's life took many turns. She was born in Russia and then moved to the United States. She worked for Jewish rights in schools there. Later, Meir got married and moved to Israel.

Golda Meir

Meir worked in politics. She helped make Israel its own country. She solved work and housing problems. Then, she worked with other countries to make things better in the world. In 1969, she became the first female leader of Israel. She was called the prime minister. She fought for Israel's rights. That is what she did for most of her life.

Women Rule!

Women have run countries all around the world. They include Costa Rica, Denmark, and Thailand. Germany has had a female leader, too, Angela Merkel (right). She is called the chancellor (CHAN-suh-luhr). Titles for leaders are not the same. But leading is a big job in every country.

Women Who Overcame

Two women stand out because they faced challenges in life. And they won!

Rosa Parks

Imagine you start your day like normal. But, at the end of the day, you change the world. That is what Rosa Parks did in 1955 in Alabama.

The bus that Parks was arrested on is on display at a museum.

Back then, African Americans could not sit with white people on buses. Black people had to sit in the back. If the bus was full, they had to stand.

One day, Parks was going home from work. She would not give up her seat to a white man. She was arrested. African Americans chose to **boycott** the buses.

A King and a Hero

You may have heard of someone who helped with the bus boycott. His name is Dr. Martin Luther King Jr. He was a **civil rights** legend.

People went on a bus strike for 381 days. That is more than a year. The **U.S. Supreme Court** heard the case. It ruled that all people could sit wherever they wanted on buses. Alabama changed its laws. This boycott was an important event in the fight for civil rights in the country.

Parks had been involved with civil rights most of her life. This time, it made her a legend.

Parks receives an award from then President Bill Clinton.

Wilma Rudolph

Wilma Rudolph was famous for never giving up. She was very sick when she was young. She wore a brace on her left leg so she could walk. Still, she had dreams of being an athlete.

Wilma Rudolph

By the time Rudolph started high school, she was much stronger. She did not need the brace on her leg. She even played sports.

One sport Rudolph showed a special talent in was track. She was fast. In 1956, she was in her first Olympic Games. She won the bronze medal in a relay race. She was only 16 years old! Four years later, Rudolph won three gold medals in one Olympic Games. She was the first woman from the United States to do so.

Wilma Rudolph

She showed both boys and girls the power of chasing their dreams. Even when things are hard, do not give up.

Going for the Gold!

Larisa Latynina (la-TIH-nee-nuh) has the most Olympic medals of any woman. She has 18! She won them in gymnastics. There is only one person in the world with more medals. U.S. swimmer Michael Phelps has 28.

Girl Power!

You have learned about some incredible women. Women have come a long way from not being allowed to vote. Now, people are voting for women to run governments. Women are leaders around the world. They lead countries. They lead companies.

Before they were leaders, they were girls. If you are a girl, what will you do to change the world? If you are a boy, how will you help the girls you know do great things? It is never too early to start working toward your dreams!

Draw It!

Draw a picture of an amazing woman. Under your drawing, write at least two sentences. Write about what she does to help or inspire others.

My nana is amazing
because she is an engineer.
She uses her imagination
to solve problems.

Glossary

boycott—stop using or supporting something

civil rights—idea that people of all religions and races should be treated fairly

Civil War—a war fought in the United States from 1861 through 1865

elements—building blocks for matter

inspired—made someone want to create or do something

leukemia—a type of cancer of the blood

natural disasters—sudden events in nature that can cause damage

Nobel Prize—one of six prizes given out each year to people for important work

noble—having qualities others admire

radiation—a strong energy that can sometimes be dangerous

U.S. Supreme Court—the highest court in the United States

Index

Your Turn!

Stamp of Approval

Wilma Rudolph had a stamp made in her honor in 2004. Choose one of the other women in this book. Design a stamp about her. What words and pictures would you use to honor her and what she did?